An unidentified 'Peak' crosses Saddleworth Viaduct, near to the summit of the former London & North Western Railway's trans-Pennine route, with the 14.05 Liverpool Lime Street-Scarborough on 22nd February 1986.

Trans-Pennine Rail Routes

L. A. Nixon

Oxford Publishing Co.

A FOULIS-OPC Railway Book

© 1988 Dr. L. Nixon & Haynes Publishing Group

British Library Cataloguing in Publication Data
Nixon, Les
  Trans-Pennine rail routes.
  1. England. Pennines. Railway services,
history.
  I. Title.
  385'. 09428

  ISBN 0-86093-307-5

Library of Congress catalog card number
88-82509

Published by:
Haynes Publishing Group
Sparkford, Near Yeovil, Somerset. BA22 7JJ

Haynes Publications Inc.
861 Lawrence Drive, Newbury Park, California 91320, USA.

Contents

Introduction

Railways are in the blood of my family, both my father and grandfather and several uncles have together more than a hundred years of railway service to their credit. Although my profession is a break with tradition, it is perhaps natural that I should have taken a keen interest in railways. My recollections now span the best part of 45 years, a period of unparalleled contraction and change in the railway industry.

As a native of South Yorkshire most of my early memories are of coal trains, hauled by steam locomotives taxed to the limit, on the long slogs across the Pennines. My local line was the former Great Central route from Wath over Woodhead to Cheshire and Lancashire. Clear in my mind even today are the queues of four or five trains waiting at the foot of Worsborough Bank for banking assistance to Penistone.

Eventually a move to North Derbyshire brought an equally intimate knowledge of the former Midland lines through Millers Dale and the Hope Valley; routes so very different to the bleak forbidding character of Woodhead. So developed a consuming interest in railways and in particular those across the Pennines; surely one of the more fascinating aspects of our English railway heritage.

Most of the lines were conceived as prime movers of freight traffic between industrialised Yorkshire and Lancashire. Lucrative freight traffic more than adequately justified the sometimes colossal civil engineering expense of promoting railways through some of the most difficult terrain in the country. Indeed, in spite of the necessity to build further tunnels the Standedge line was eventually quadrupled between Huddersfield and Stalybridge while a significant portion of the Woodhead line acquired a four track facility. How different though were the sharp curves, gradients and altitudes of the Cromford and High Peak and the rural railway through Wensleydale to Hawes and Garsdale. In this album I have sought to compare and contrast the character of all of the trans-Pennine railways, past and present.

The story commences with the London & North Western Railway's Ashbourne-Buxton-Manchester and Cromford and High Peak lines in the south and concludes in the north with another pioneering trans-Pennine route, the former North Eastern Railway connection between Newcastle and Carlisle. In each case the reader is taken on a pictorial journey starting on the eastern side of the Pennines.

Clearly it was not possible, nor was it the intention, to fully document the history and development of the ten trans-Pennine railways. The photographs are therefore mainly contemporary but with interesting references to the age of steam.

Numerous authoritative works on the subject have been published over the years, and the author will be well pleased if the visual appeal of this volume prompts a deeper interest and enthusiasm for what is arguably the finest railway route mileage south of the border.

In preparing this volume I have become only too aware of the deficiencies of my collection and I would record my grateful thanks to those photographers who have contributed valuable photographs to help plug some of the more obvious gaps.

Inevitably, in the space available I have only been able to offer a distillation of the character of these railways and although some readers will identify omissions my hope is that this will not significantly detract from their enjoyment.

L.A. Nixon
Hathersage.

Dedication

In memory of my father Arthur Nixon, who, as a fireman and driver, knew Woodhead intimately.

Chapter 1

Cromford and High Peak – Buxton-Stockport

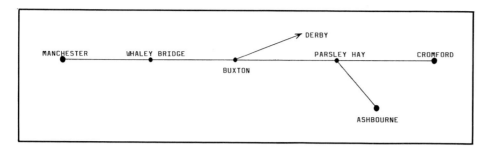

Arguably one of the more interesting gradient posts of British Rail. Photographed at the foot of Sheep Pasture incline in 1955.

(Ken Plant)

The Cromford and High Peak Railway had a chequered career of 136 years. The line was opened in 1831 and, by virtue of its numerous rope-worked inclines it became from the outset, unique among Britain's railways. The line left the Cromford Canal and the latter day Midland Railway's Derby to Manchester main line at Cromford, although much of the route mileage was situated high on the Derbyshire limestone moors, the majority at altitudes of greater than 800 ft above sea level. Following a tortuous route it eventually reached its western extremity at Whaley Bridge.

Latterly the only surviving sections were from Cromford to Parsley Hay and a three mile long branch from Brierlow to Ladmanlow. The section from Parsley Hay to Brierlow was used by the rural Ashbourne to Buxton line when this was completed in 1892. This development also made available a fairly easily graded route through Buxton to Whaley Bridge leading to the simultaneous abandonment of the CHPR Ladmanlow-Whaley Bridge section. Unlike the other trans-Pennine railways the CHPR never boasted a regular passenger service, apart from a brief period in the 1870s when a journey over the 33 mile line took a whole day.

Sunday 30th April 1967 was the date of complete closure; much of the trackbed of the Parsley Hay-Cromford and Parsley Hay-Ashbourne sections now sees recreational use as a ramblers' footpath and cycle track. The Buxton-Hindlow section survives as a branch serving Tarmac, Steetley, Peakstone and ICI industrial complexes.

The LNWR line beyond Buxton climbed steeply to a summit close to Dove Holes followed by a picturesque descent to Whaley Bridge, Hazel Grove and Stockport. The line narrowly escaped the Beeching axe and today it provides a well patronised hourly interval local service although normally all freight traffic from Buxton is routed via Peak Forest.

When built the CHPR had no fewer then seven rope-worked inclines and two, at Middleton and Sheep Pasture at the eastern end of the line, were in service until the line closed in April 1967. Each incline was worked by a stationary steam engine, (except the Sheep Pasture incline in later years), and in the interests of efficiency loaded and empty wagons were usually worked down and up the line simultaneously. The possibility of 25 ton runaway wagons down 1 in 8 inclines was a clear hazard and not surprisingly, quite rigorous precautions were taken. This wagon seems to be very securely attached to the rope as it is prepared to start the descent of Sheep Pasture incline in July 1965.

The short length of line between Sheep Pasture and Middleton inclines was worked for many years by ex LNWR 2-4-0T No. 58092 which was replaced in later years by the much more modern Kitson 0-4-0ST, some of which were built as late as 1953. Here one of the later batch, No. 47006, takes water at Sheep Pasture in July 1965.

For many years the former North London Railway 0-6-0Ts gave yeoman service between Middleton Top and Parsley Hay. Illustrated (below) is No. 58856 at Longcliffe on 21st May 1955. These handsome locomotives were ousted by the Riddles austerity J94 class 0-6-0ST which survived until closure of the line.

Hugh Ballantyne)

The 1960s was the era of dieselisation and even the CHP did not escape. There was a proposal to replace steam by standard Class 08 diesel shunters and trials were undertaken on at least one occasion. These three pictures illustrate the event on 2nd August 1965; complete closure of the line taking place just nine months later on 30th April 1967.

Top: At a height of almost 1,100 ft above sea level, Class 08 No. D3778 rounds the tight curve at Longcliffe with a very substantial train for the CHP, 13 wagons and a brake van, bound for Middleton Top. The official supervising the trials can be seen clearly through the left hand cab window.

Centre: The load was reduced to eight wagons for the cautious descent of the 1 in 14 Hopton incline.

The bleak High Peak scenery is very evident in this picture of Class J94 0-6-0ST No. 68006 crossing the unique stone embankment at Minninglow in April 1966. On this day the payload was an old tender and a guard's van.

Below left: The crews discuss the relative merits of steam and diesel as the regular and trial trains stand together at Friden. Judging by the makeshift weather protection on the cab of Class J94 0-6-0ST No. 68006, the diesel would seem favourite to win hands down – at least during the winter months!

Many would argue that the Ashbourne to Buxton line was scenically one of the finest in Britain, and certainly its stations were well patronised by hikers and ramblers, particularly on summer weekends. Stanier 2-6-4T No. 42600 and Class 4F 0-6-0 No. 44030 provided the motive power for an excursion from the East Midlands on Easter Monday 1962 and are pictured here hard at work leaving Hartington for Buxton.

(Brian Staniland)

The view looking east, of the all-timber Alsop-en-le-Dale for Alstonfield station shortly after the track had been lifted early in 1966. The trackbed continues to carry wheeled traffic to this day but unfortunately nothing more than bicycles on what is now known as the Tissington Trail. The Ashbourne-Hartington section was closed completely on 7th October 1963.

Parsley Hay, a junction in the middle of nowhere, was the meeting point of the Cromford and High Peak and the Ashbourne-Buxton lines. Before the link to Buxton was completed from Parsley Hay the CHP followed a twisting route through Hurdlow, Dowlow, Harpur Hill, Ladmanlow, and down three rope worked inclines (at Bunsall, Smallcross and Whaley Bridge) to the canal at Whaley Bridge. The new direct line into Buxton was built on part of the trackbed of the CHPR as far as Harpur Hill, but the section on to Ladmanlow was retained to service local industry. Here, Ivatt 2-6-0 No. 46401 had just joined the main line at Parsley Hay with a freight from Friden on the CHP for Buxton on 22nd April 1965.

By 1984 freight traffic over the surviving Buxton-Hindlow remnant of this scenic line had dwindled to an 'as required' afternoon freight to Briggs Sidings for ICI Hindlow, and even these trains frequently loaded to only three or four wagons. Certainly the one wagon payload behind Class 40 No. 40192 on 5th January 1984 was hardly a viable economic proposition.

Photographed from the same viewpoint, this picture taken some 20 years earlier makes an interesting comparison. A much tidier railway scene greets Class 8F 2-8-0 No. 48532 arriving from Buxton with a string of empty five-plank wagons.

Workmen get to grips with the demolition of the station buildings at Hindlow in the early Spring of 1966. Looking down the track in the Ashbourne direction, Hindlow Tunnel can be seen.

With the cessation of active quarrying at the ICI complex at Hindlow, a contract was signed with BR to ship limestone from the major quarry at Tunstead on a seven-days-a-week basis. A development which secures the immediate future at least of this interesting branch. To mark the event a naming ceremony was held at Hindlow Works on 23rd June 1988. Immaculate Class 37/5 No. 37688 was formally named *Great Rocks* by three ICI employees. Here, the locomotive, along with No. 37380, eases hoppers through the unloader immediately after the unveiling ceremony.

The ICI lime burners at Hindlow were coal fired for many years, which along with oil for the nearby Dowlow Steetly works, provided BR with valuable revenue. In this scene, 'Peak' class No. 45013 is pictured near Harpur Hill with a lengthy train of empties on 1st June 1978. These trains have not run for a number of years since the conversion of the plants at Hindlow to burn natural gas.

Apart from that used by the Ashbourne-Buxton line, a short section of the CHP alignment to Whaley Bridge west of Parsley Hay was in use until closure in 1967. The three mile branch left the Ashbourne line at Brierlow, the summit (1,268 ft above sea level) and the highest point reached by a railway in Derbyshire. The branch served Government installations and quarries at Harpur Hill and Ladmanlow. On 27th June 1953 an SLS/MLS tour traversed the whole of the surviving CHP line. Here Class 3F 0-6-0 No. 43387 runs round its train at the end of the branch. Note the LNWR cast iron noticeboard at the bottom left of the picture.

(Ken Plant)

Above: A notable first visit to Buxton occurred on 8th February 1986 when snow drifts up to six feet in depth greeted "Hoover" No. 50012 *Benbow* with the "Derbyshire Dingle" railtour. Even local railwaymen braved the weather and turned out with their cameras – note the gentleman in action immediately to the left of the signal box, as the train leaves for Stockport and Manchester Piccadilly.

Below: Awaiting their next turn of duty on the centre road are Class 20s Nos 20085 and 20041 flanked by Class 104 and 108 dmus, on a very cold 13th January 1985.

The Midland and the London & North Western Railways built terminal stations alongside each other at Buxton and both were still in use until the mid-1960s. Pictured here is BR standard Class 5 4-6-0 No. 73140 (with Caprotti valve gear) standing at the Midland side buffer stops after arrival with a ramblers' excursion from Nottingham and Derby on 7th July 1962. This station has now been completely demolished, but fortunately a fan window identical to the one seen here has been retained in the surviving adjacent ex LNWR station.

(Brian Staniland)

For many years Midland 0-4-4Ts operated the shuttle service between Buxton and Millers Dale but, inevitably, they were later replaced by the ubiquitous diesel multiple unit. In this scene, now of particular interest as the site is being actively redeveloped by the Peak Railway Society, single car unit No. M79964 (Waggon and Maschinenbau of West Germany, 1958) leaves Buxton Midland in the Autumn of 1966. This vehicle is now preserved and is operated on the Keighley & Worth Valley Railway.

(Martin Welch)

Class 20s Nos 20111 and 20165 struggle uphill near Combs with empty hoppers for Tunstead on 16th June 1985.

West of Buxton the LNWR line to Whaley Bridge and Stockport has not carried regular freight traffic for many years. Very occasionally, when the normal route via Peak Forest is closed because of engineering work, the line is pressed into use. Such was the case in 1984 when the construction of a new road bypass around Chapel-en-le-Frith closed the Midland line on a number of weekends.

Opposite top: Class 20s Nos 20172 and 20077 find themselves in unfamiliar territory on Sunday 9th September 1984 as they head away from Buxton with an ICI Tunstead-Northwich stone train.

Opposite bottom: The curve linking the former Midland and London & North Western routes at Hazel Grove was brought into use with the introduction of the Summer 1986 timetable. In this study, Class 31/4 No. 31424 joins the ex LNWR Buxton line with the 11.22 Sheffield-Liverpool on 14th June 1986.

Chapter 2

Derby - Ambergate - Peak Forest - Manchester

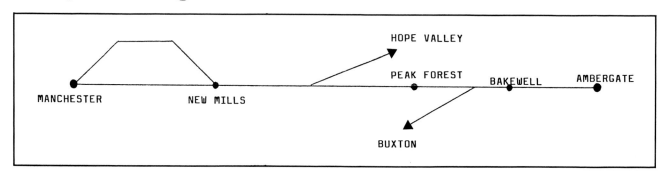

The Midland Railway's major bid for a significant share in the wealth generated by the Lancashire industrial belt came to fruition with the completion of its independent route to Manchester in 1867. The railway, one of the most scenic in Britain, diverged from the direct Derby-Chesterfield line at Ambergate in a north westerly direction passing through Matlock, Bakewell, Peak Forest (summit at 980ft above sea level), Chinley and Disley to reach a superb station at Manchester Central. Topography dictated that the railway by-passed Buxton but the town was served by a branch from Millers Dale which diverged from the mainline just north of Chee Tor and Rusher Cutting tunnels at Millers Dale Junction. The branch then followed the narrow confines of Ashwood Dale to Buxton; an impressive 5^1/2 mile journey.

Freight traffic over the route was quite intensive even in the early 1960s; Rowsley was the nerve centre of freight operation in the east whereas the somewhat isolated yard at Gowhole was the Midland's focal point for local freight movements to Lancashire and Cheshire.

Civil engineering works on the line were considerable, being both expensive to construct and to maintain. Like its near neighbour to the south, the Cromford and High Peak, the line was closed as a through route in 1967. A branch was retained at Ambergate to serve Matlock while the line to the north of Peak Forest Junction, and the branch up Ashwood Dale was kept to serve local quarries such as the giant ICI complex at Tunstead, and to provide an alternative route into Buxton.

The long term objective of the Peak Rail Society, based at Buxton and Matlock, is to reinstate the rail link between the two towns.

In recent times the prestige train of the line was undoubtedly the "Midland Pullman" offering an attractive, if not particularly fast service, between Manchester and St. Pancras. Certainly for many passengers the extra 38 minutes required for the journey compared with the more direct LNW route was more than compensated by the superb scenery of the Peak District. In this Summer 1962 scene the Metro-Cammell built train speeds through Ambergate forming an evening 'down' service.

(Brian Staniland)

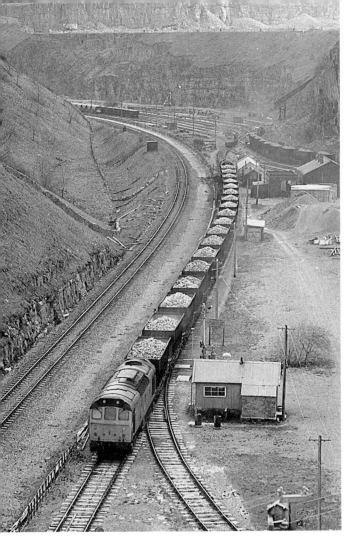

The ICI quarries at Tunstead generate a significant income for the Freight Sector of British Rail. The magnitude of the operation can be appreciated in this general scene which features Class 25 No. 25170 leaving with a loaded train for Northwich on 9th April 1981. A further Class 25 can just be seen banking the train, while a Class 40 lurks in the yard waiting its next turn of duty.

Ambergate was once a major junction of the Midland Railway and one of the few places where station platforms were provided on all three faces of a triangle of lines. The station remains open for business but it has been reduced to a single unstaffed platform servicing trains on the single line Matlock branch. In days gone by, for Manchester bound passengers, Ambergate marked the commencement of the trans-Pennine journey; scenically one which was second only to the Settle and Carlisle route. Sadly, enthusiasts on the "Class 58 Pioneer" railtour were limited to a journey over the surviving Matlock-Ambergate section, but at least the motive power was unusual, indeed it was the first passenger duty for a class 58. No. 58002 prepares to rejoin the main line at Ambergate on the return working on 18th September 1983.

Opposite: Presenting the 1985 image, a 3-car Class 151 dmu No. 151001 heads away from Matlock Bath with the 11.05 Matlock-Derby service on 20th December. In the middle distance can be seen one of the pylons and the control centre for the new and popular cable car to the Heights of Abraham.

Apart from occasional excursion traffic, locomotive hauled movements over the Matlock branch are few and far between. One regular working is the annual weedkilling train which in 1980 was powered by Class 25 No. 25135 seen here passing Matlock station on 24th June.

Even though the platform awnings on the 'up' platform have been demolished, there can be little doubting the Midland ancestry of the station at Bakewell. A 3-car Craven's dmu forming a Derby-Manchester service makes a leisurely departure in July 1966. The station buildings survive intact although the space between the platforms has been filled in with rubble. Much of the goods yard and part of the former main line trackbed is now used as a small industrial estate, although sufficient room to accommodate a single line remains should the aspirations of the Peak Railway Society to link Matlock and Buxton become a reality.

Hassop was a tiny station strangely located just one mile to the north of Bakewell and well over one mile away from the hamlet of that name. It was the station used by the Duke of Devonshire, whereas Bakewell was patronised by the Duke of Rutland. Since Hassop boasted a population of around 70 persons it is certain that their contribution to passenger receipts must have been minimal and the closure of the station in August 1942 was inevitable. Here, on a dull day in March 1965, a 'Peak' approaches the station with a 'down' express. The 'down' sidings, regularly used to loop slow moving freight trains climbing to Peak Forest, are clearly visible.

Above: Visitors to the remains of Millers Dale station, currently in use as local National Park ranger headquarters, would be hard pressed to recognise this view of the north end taken on 6th October 1958. A Class 101 Metro-Cammell dmu is pictured arriving from Buxton. Note the Midland lower quadrant dolly signals.

(*Martin Welch*)

Opposite top: In a canyon location reminiscent of the wild west of America rather than the Peak District, a 'down' St Pancras-Manchester express with 'Peak' No. D128 in charge, raises the echoes as it approaches Peak Forest Junction in April 1965. Today the quarry works and the signal box have totally disappeared and while the main line to the south of this point is now lifted, a single track connection from Great Rocks Junction through Ashwood Dale to Buxton has been retained.

Opposite bottom: The civil engineering feature of the Midland main line, which is as familiar to casual visitors as it is to railway enthusiasts, is the superb viaduct over the River Wye in Monsal Dale. It now features prominently in National Park publicity material, but when built is was considered by many to be an "awful blemish" on the beautiful Peak landscape. In this rather unusual view an unidentified Class 45 bursts out of Headstone Tunnel and on to the viaduct with a 'down' express for Manchester Central in April 1965.

Right: The triangle of lines, bounded by the Buxton, Peak Forest and Millers Dale Junction signal boxes were located in a spectacular ravine of the River Wye some three miles to the east of Buxton. Today only the single line curve linking Wye and Great Rocks Dale survives, seen here being negotiated by a freight train double headed by a Class 25 and a Class 37. Just visible above the rear of the train is the remains of one of the smallest stations in Britain, Blackwell Halt. The low platforms, long enough to accommodate just one coach, were built for the benefit of company employees resident in cottages built in the triangle.

Below: Making the very last appearance of steam on a freight train in the Hope Valley is Class 8F 2-8-0 No. 48191 struggling westbound up Norman's Bank with a loaded cement train on 2nd May 1968. The train was making such slow progress that it was possible to chase the train successfully on a pedal cycle.

Opposite: The bleak and forbidding moorland plateau of Kinder Scout dominates the scenery of upper Edale where snow frequently lingers on the uppermost slopes until May. By comparison the railway and its trains assume an almost model-like appearance typified in this view of a Class 124 Trans-Pennine unit forming the 14.15 Sheffield-Manchester Piccadilly on 4th May 1981. Close to this point is the start of the Pennine Way footpath by which route the Woodhead line at Torside is only ten miles distant.

A photograph which epitomises the problems of building trans-Pennine railways. Class 47 No. 47583 slogs up the 1 in 100 from Chinley East towards Cowburn Tunnel and the summit with the 15.15 Manchester Piccadilly-Harwich Parkeston Quay on 2nd May 1983.

The western portal of Cowburn Tunnel is best seen in spring before the trees develop their full complement of leaves. The two mile 182 yard long tunnel marks the summit of the line at around 900 ft. During construction work in the early 1890s a tramway was built from a point to the left of the tunnel mouth to the top of Toot Hill for the sinking of ventilation shafts. A Craven's dmu bound for Sheffield was photographed here on 20th March 1976.

Opposite top: At the time of writing the Class 31/4s are the mainstay of motive power for the Hope Valley trans-Pennine services. Not surprisingly they are complete masters of the usual featherweight four-coach consist typified here by No. 31430 eastbound at Edale, with the 10.41 Manchester Piccadilly-Sheffield on 27th November 1985.

Opposite bottom: After an absence of almost 20 years a Stanier 8F 2-8-0 made a spectacular return to the Hope Valley line on 24th October 1987. Here, an immaculate No. 48151, recently restored to main line standards by the Midland Railway Trust at Butterley, revives memories of their former exploits in the Peak District as it storms away from an Edale stop with a Derby-Buxton excursion loaded to twelve bogies.

These days it is a rare occasion to refer to a newly laid section of BR track, but happily this is the case for the link between Chinley South and Chinley East Junctions. The line, which enabled 'down' trains from the Derby direction to gain direct access to the Hope Valley, was declared redundant and lifted in 1966, but was reinstated as a single line in 1981. In this study 'Peak' No. 45122 joins the Hope Valley route at Chinley East with a mineral train from Tunstead quarries on 1st September 1983.

The photograph (below) presents a view of the junction in March 1965 where the former Midland Railway signal box and gantry of lower quadrants can be seen clearly. An unidentified Class 47 with a westbound football excursion takes the line to Chinley North, where today a modern signal box controls all movements over the triangle of lines at Chinley.

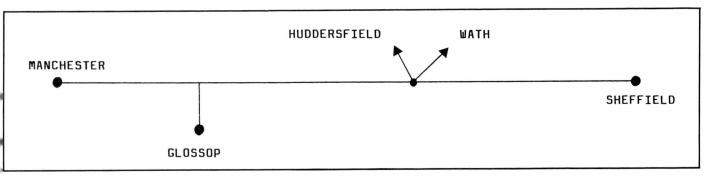

MANCHESTER   GLOSSOP   HUDDERSFIELD   WATH   SHEFFIELD

Chapter 4

The Woodhead Route

The Woodhead line in its heyday was one of the busiest trans-Pennine routes, second only to Standedge just a few miles to the north. In the east there were two focal points, both in South Yorkshire. Sheffield was the springboard to the East Midlands and London via the Great Central, while the freight only branch to Wath Yard in the heart of the South Yorkshire coalfield was the point of origin of vast numbers of coal trains destined for Lancashire and Cheshire.

The fortunes of the line parallel the rise and dramatic fall of coal traffic. Even as late as the early 1950s the future of the line seemed very rosy indeed. At the time, many might have argued that if rationalisation of the trans-Pennine railways had to be contemplated in the future, then surely Woodhead would be one of the last to succumb. Vast sums were invested in the construction of a new tunnel and electrification at 1,500 volt dc. An electrified trans-Pennine line was, at the time, hailed as a railway of the future. But sadly, in less than a life time it became a non standard thorn in the side of an expanding 25kV network. Rapidly dwindling freight traffic could not justify the expense of conversion and so in 1981, after an electrified life of only 27 years it passed into history.

The line is unique in other respects, not least the forbidding bleak moorland scenery; characterful certainly but arguably one of the least attractive routes across the Pennines.

Like its LNW counterpart at Standedge no fewer than three tunnels were constructed between the summit at Dunford Bridge and Woodhead. The two single bores were ready to receive trains in 1845 and 1852 but, unlike Standedge, the third double bore was completed over a century later in 1953. An event which was coincident with the closure of both nineteenth century tunnels.

The section to the west of Hadfield, along with the branch to Glossop, has been retained but converted to the standard 25kV system, and provides a vital contribution to the suburban rail network of Greater Manchester.

At the eastern end a single line survives to service the British Steel Works at Stocksbridge. Just beyond Deepcar the route of the line is now permanently breeched by the new Stocksbridge road link to the M1 Motorway.

Emerging from the stygian gloom of Woodhead Tunnel are Class 76 Nos 76021 and 76025 with a merry-go-round coal haul for Fiddler's Ferry Power Station on 14th May 1981.

The topsy turvy fragmented freight facilities of the Sheffield area were rationalised in the early 1960s with the construction of Tinsley Yard. The mammoth project was completed in 1965 with an official opening on 29th October. In this March 1966 scene Class 13 No. D4582 straddles the hump while in the distance can be seen Class 25 and 31 diesels and an 8F class steam locomotive. The combination of two Class 08 shunters to create a new Class 13 locomotive was the neat solution to the hump shunting motive power problem. Initially, master and slave units were coupled together cab to cab, as seen here, but this arrangement was soon modified by turning the master unit around to improve visibility. The 1,500 volt dc catenary giving access to Woodhead traffic is visible on the left.

July 17th 1981 was the last day of through trains using the Woodhead line, and while it was to be two years before some track lifting commenced, the task of removing overhead wire and fittings was soon completed. A pair of Class 20s, with No. 20008 leading, swings away from the GC main line under the de-wired catenary at Woodburn Junction, to the east of Sheffield Victoria, and prepare to negotiate Attercliffe Junction with a Deepcar-Tinsley trip working on 1st December 1982.

In the days when Sheffield Victoria boasted a Pullman service to King's Cross, Class 40 No. D206 (40006), without the unflattering yellow warning panels, waits departure in July 1960.

Sheffield Victoria in an advanced state of decay. It is hard to appreciate its once-vital role servicing trains for Manchester, Bradford, Barnsley, Doncaster, Retford, Nottingham and beyond. Today, not a single passenger train passes through but in the early 1980s the route was used by local trains to Penistone and Huddersfield. Here, a Calder Valley Class 110 dmu forming the 11.38 Sheffield-Huddersfield disturbs the funereal silence on 29th July 1980.

In 1970 the last scheduled passenger train called at Sheffield Victoria, but another 14 years were to elapse before the tracks through the station were finally lifted. Class 20 No. 20040 provided the power for the track lifting train on 4th July 1984 – a dubious honour indeed. In the Summer of 1987 part of the site was used for the construction of an extension to the adjoining Royal Victoria Hotel.

Opposite top: A 2-car Class 101 Metro-Cammell dmu rattles down the hill near Wadsley Bridge, forming a Huddersfield-Sheffield via Penistone service on 13th May 1983. At one time Neepsend Power Station received supplies of coal by rail and the area seen here to the right of the main line accommodated an extensive fan of sidings.

Opposite bottom: Wadsley Bridge station has been used for many years as the most convenient railhead for football excursion passengers bound for the Hillsborough ground of Sheffield Wednesday. Class 76 Nos 76032 and 76034 take the heavy Broughton Lane-Ditton, British Oxygen Co. train past the station and through the yard at Wadsley Bridge on 7th July 1981, a few days before complete closure of the line as a through trans-Pennine route. The section between Sheffield Victoria and Deepcar has been retained to service the BSC works at Stocksbridge. On the right is Class 08 No. 08022.

Above: Until 1981 Wath Yard was one of three Eastern Region freight terminal points of the Woodhead line. On 23rd September 1981 Class 37 No. 37019 and a pair of Class 20s wait their turn to depart with eastbound trains. Today, all trace of the 1,500 volt dc catenary, visible here in the distance, has been removed, along with all of the track.

The introduction of the Class 141 4-wheel railbuses to the local services operated in the West Yorkshire PTE area has been less than a total success, but at least the cream and green livery was a welcome visual change from the usual BR blue. Unit No. 141010 is pictured in the bay platform at the east end of Huddersfield station early in the morning of 10th February 1985.

The interesting track layout at Springwood Junction, Huddersfield is negotiated by Class 40 with a freight bound for Lancashire in October 1965. The tracks diverging to the right are the connections to the Penistone branch.

A scene which poignantly emphasises the contraction which has taken place on Britain's railways. It is difficult to visualise the once-complicated fan of sidings, goods sheds and coal drops which used to occupy this now vacant site at Paddock. 'Peak' No. 45062 passes with an express for Liverpool on 25th July 1981.

A view of the Colne Valley, which epitomises the character of the West Riding of Yorkshire. A 2-car dmu forming the 10.50 Leeds-Marsden crosses Longwood Viaduct against a backdrop of gaunt moorland, mill chimneys and terraced houses on 21st January 1984. Many of the Victorian woollen mills in the area are now being demolished and the one on the right has not escaped the march of progress.

The swansong of the 'Deltics' before their final withdrawal at the end of 1981 was undoubtedly their appearance on York-Liverpool services. In the closing months of the year they were regular performers on the 08.50 ex York and the 13.05 return working from Liverpool. With the usual featherweight seven-coach train in tow, immaculate No. 55009 *Alicydon* approaches Springwood Junction, Huddersfield with the 13.05 departure from Liverpool on 11th November 1981.

Following the closure of the Woodhead line in July 1981 trans-Pennine merry-go-round coal hauls to Fiddler's Ferry Power Station were routed over the Standedge line; a move which brought Class 56s to the line on a regular basis. Approaching Springwood Junction, Huddersfield is No. 56030 with a string of empty HAAs on 11th November 1981.

During the ten days before the Christmas of 1981, Britain experienced some of the coldest weather in living memory. On the railways frozen points, locomotive fuel lines and radiators were just a few of the many operational problems. Here nine inches of snow cling precariously to the roofs of a row of terraced houses at Golcar near Huddersfield, as Class 47 No. 47411 passes by 50 minutes late with the 09.50 York-Liverpool express on 17th December.

Opposite top: In 1965 all four tracks up the Colne Valley were in use, but the level of traffic had declined to a point where rationalisation was inevitable. 3-car Class 101 dmu forming a local service for Manchester accelerates away from Linthwaite on a dull and damp November day, just 18 months before two of the lines were lifted.

Opposite bottom: For many years in the late 1960s, '70s and early '80s the Class 123/124 units were synonymous with InterCity services across the Pennines; initially on the Standedge line but latterly on the Hope Valley route. On a very wet day in October 1965 a Trans Pennine unit in green livery approaches Marsden, forming an eastbound service for Leeds. Note the water column at the far end of the weed-ridden platform.

The stamping ground of Foggy, Cleggy and Compo? There can be little doubting the Yorkshire character of this scene depicting Class 47 approaching the Standedge twin bore tunnel at Marsden on a dull July day in 1982. Clearly visible is the loop, the only remnant of the quadruple track surviving east of the summit.

Right: It is interesting to compare this photograph with that which introduces this Chapter on page 70. Today no trace remains of Diggle station, but in the Summer of 1967 it was still intact, albeit rather neglected and still with gas lamps in situ. From a weed strewn platform 1 a porter watches Class 5 4-6-0 No. 44971 gallop through with an eastbound SO holiday train.

The hard work over, a Class 45/1 'Peak' hurries down the hill from Diggle towards Saddleworth with the 12.55 Scarborough-Bangor on 22nd February 1986.

The Brush Class 31s are quite infrequent visitors to the Standedge line, but it is doubtful whether the football fan passengers of this train appreciated their good fortune when No. 31402 was rostered for their Huddersfield bound train on 9th January 1985! The unusual number of spectators on the footbridge to the west of Diggle were waiting to photograph the following train, a steam hauled SLOA special for York.

One of the best known viaducts on the Standedge line is that at Saddleworth, crossed here by Class 31 No. 31253 with the diverted Heaton-Red Bank empty newspaper train on 2nd September 1978. With 18 vehicles in tow, the 1,500 hp Brush must have made a particularly sluggish ascent of the 1 in 105 gradients of the Colne Valley. Other noteworthy features are the surviving Saddleworth station buildings seen to the left of the rear of the train, and the single arch bridge at the bottom left which until 1955 carried branch trains to Delph.

Five degrees of frost, three inches of snow and bright sunshine combine to afford a spectacular setting for Class 47 No. 47535 eastbound near Uppermill on New Year's Day 1980. The train is approaching Saddleworth Viaduct and the site of the junction for the erstwhile branch line to Delph.

Opposite top: In sub-zero temperatures No. 55022 *Royal Scots Grey* rounds the curve eastbound between Saddleworth and Diggle Junction on 17th December 1981. The train, a very mixed five-coach scratch consist, forming the 13.05 Liverpool-York, was running almost one hour late because of extensive delays to the balance working from Yorkshire. Until the mid 1960s the signal gantry carried an additional distant signal relating to the now lifted 'down' line through the single bore tunnel at Standedge.

Opposite middle: Each winter the roads across the Pennines are, from time to time, blocked by snow and on these occasions the only sensible way to travel between Lancashire and Yorkshire is by train. Certainly wise advice on 17th December 1981 when the photographer had some difficulty getting home after taking this picture at Diggle of a Class 47 heading the 14.05 Liverpool-York.

Opposite bottom: On New Year's Eve 1979 non-boilered English Electric Class 40 No. 40193 at the head of a block oil train, passes Greenfield Junction on the eastbound climb to Diggle. The trackbed of the now closed and lifted LNW line to Lees and Oldham can be seen to the right of the locomotive; once a lucrative intrusion into L&Y territory.

The narrow confines of the valley of the River Tame is particularly evident in this study of Scout Tunnel to the south of Mossley. In the days when "Whistlers" were regular performers on passenger trains on the line No. 40153 heads the 09.10 Scarborough-Llandudno towards Stalybridge on 30th June 1979. At the foot of the housing estate at the top right of the picture is an embankment marking the route of the Friezland loop.

A picture which completely captures the character of the trans-Pennine railway is this study of Class 47 No. 47632 negotiating the sinuous curves between Mossley and Greenfield Junction, with the 14.03 Liverpool-Scarborough on 26th April 1986.

Immediately ahead of 'Whistler' No. 40033 formerly D233 *Empress of England* is the strangely named Horsefall Tunnel just to the east of Hall Royd Junction, Todmorden. The 18 bogies of the morning empty Red Bank newspaper train curve out of sight. The milepost, visible above the locomotive, reminds the driver that he has another 20 miles to cover to journey's end at Manchester.

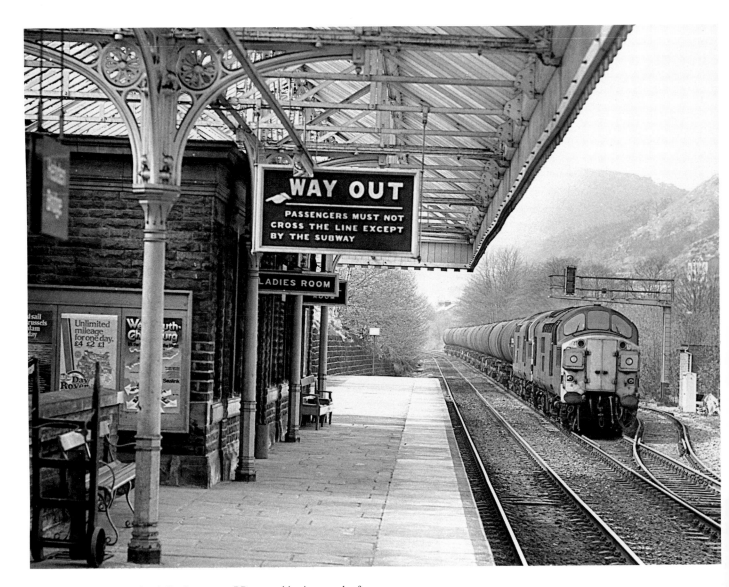

Hebden Bridge station belies its present BR ownership since much of the original Lancashire & Yorkshire Railway architecture and appointments remain to this day. However, the Day Rover advertisment, the colour light signalling, and of course the English Electric Class 37s, present the modern face of trans-Pennine railways. Nos 37096 and 37045 head an eastbound oil train on 20th April 1982.

Coasting down the 1 in 182 from Todmorden with a freight for Healey Mills on 21st April 1982 is 'Peak' No. 45040. Millwood Tunnel can be seen in the middle distance.

Opposite top: The pleasant rural scenery of the southbound climb to Copy Pit Summit is in marked contrast to the terraced houses and mills which cling to the steep-sided valley between Portsmouth and Todmorden. The outskirts of Burnley and Pendle Hill provide the backdrop for the 13.30 SO Blackpool-Castleford; a 9-car dmu formation comprising two 3- car Metro-Cammell units and a 3-car BRCW Class 110 unit, on 24th July 1982.

Opposite bottom: Surprisingly, Portsmouth is in Lancashire but it is a long way from the sea. This train, the SO 09.27 Sheffield-Blackpool climbs towards "Pompey" – red rose style – amid mill chimneys and moorland scenery on 14th August 1982 with No. 37122 in charge

Above: In home territory, a Calder Valley Class 110 dmu forming a Halifax-Manchester service is seen shortly after leaving Todmorden on the climb to Walsden and Summit Tunnel on 18th August 1981.

Right: Discounting the Newcastle & Carlisle, the Calder Valley line was the first major trans-Pennine railway, and the least steeply graded of them all. Once trains have reached Newton Heath on the climb out of Manchester Victoria the steepest grade is a very modest half mile of 1 in 126 near Moston. Not surprisingly the heaviest Lancashire-Yorkshire freights, including lucrative oil traffic, are now routed over the L&Y.

Class 47 No. 47303 eases a train of oil tankers downgrade through Walsden on 20th August 1981.

Opposite top: Almost until the end of steam, bankers were maintained at Todmorden to assist freight trains up the bank to the summit of Copy Pit. Here, two 8Fs, photographed from Stansfield Hall Junction, wait patiently for a call to duty just before Christmas 1966.

Opposite bottom: Todmorden is spectacularly situated at the meeting point of three valleys cut by ice-age glaciers. The Lancashire & Yorkshire main line follows the two southernmost valleys, while the third accommodates the connection to Burnley over Copy Pit Summit. A triangle of lines permitted the movement of trains in all directions; the western junction was paradoxically known as Todmorden East and the northern junction, Stansfield Hall. In 1983 only the eastern junction, Hall Royd, remained and is the location for this picture of Class 37 No. 37215 taking the Burnley line with the 09.22 summer Saturday only Sheffield-Blackpool express on 14th August 1982.

A concrete facsimile of the 1950's BR lion and wheel emblem still in situ on the northern platform of Todmorden station in December 1984.

In December 1984 the Calder Valley line hit the national headlines when an oil train became derailed and caught fire in Summit Tunnel. For a time the future of the L&Y main line seemed in doubt, but repairs were succesfully completed in the Summer of 1985. Class 46 No. 46008 heads the empty Heaton-Red Bank empty newspaper train out of the western portal on 20th August 1981.

The snow covered Pennines provide a spectacular backdrop to this picture of a Calder Valley Class 110 dmu forming the 15.15 Manchester Victoria-Leeds, seen approaching Rochdale East Junction on 26th February 1977.

Preserved ex Midland Railway, Compound No. 1000 climbs away from Red Bank carriage sidings towards Thorpe Bridges Junction, Newton Heath with the empty stock of a return Rochdale-York private charter on 26th February 1983. Despite her age and the substantial seven-coach train, the 4-4-0 turned in a faultless performance on the Calder Valley line. Visible above the train is the Manchester Victoria-Bury electrified line.

Rochdale East Junction marks the northern end of the loop line serving Shaw and Oldham, whereas the southern connection is at Thorpe Bridges Junction close to Newton Heath TMD. Today the loop line rarely sees locomotive hauled trains, multiple units forming the circular service to Manchester Victoria, augmented by a direct shuttle through Oldham to Shaw. These two scenes show the loop line in recent years.

Above: Football excursion traffic brings the occasional diesel locomotive to Oldham. Bringing Newcastle United fans into Oldham (Werneth) station from the Manchester direction on 31st December 1983, is 'Peak' No. 45015. The bridge in the middle distance marks the location of the junction with the line to the L&Y main line at Middleton Junction. Since this stretch included the notorious 1 mile long 1 in 27 Werneth Bank it is not surprising that it was closed and lifted many years ago.

197

Below: A Class 104 unit from Manchester approaches a deserted Oldham (Mumps) station. In its heyday this was a major railway centre with extensive goods yards occupying the waste ground at the left of the picture.

Trains to Royton and Rochdale →

Chapter 7

Leeds - Skipton - Carnforth and Preston

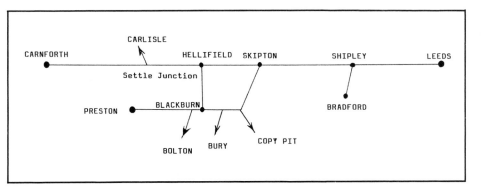

This chapter covers a selection of trans-Pennine routes located in North Yorkshire where the Leeds-Skipton section is common to all. At the latter point a southerly line served Colne and the other north east Lancashire cotton towns, eventually being joined by the Copy Pit link from the Calder Valley route at Gannow Junction, Burnley. Further west came Accrington, Blackburn (with a trailing junction from Hellifield), and eventually connection with the West Coast Main Line at Preston. Further lines to south Lancashire diverged at Accrington (to Bury) and at Blackburn (to Bolton).

The northern option at Skipton traverses pleasant undulating Yorkshire Dales scenery through Hellifield where it is joined by the line from Blackburn. A little further to the west the Settle and Carlisle line diverges to take its separate northwards way at Settle Junction. In contrast with the other trans-Pennine lines none of these routes are characterised by clearly defined summits; Eldroth marks the modest summit to the east of Settle Junction. From here the line takes a falling grade to the WCML at Carnforth.

Scenically all are rather nondescript, with perhaps the industrial sections between Colne and Blackburn and the West Riding having the greatest appeal. Modest gradients and minimal civil engineering works complete a picture of a rather uninspiring selection of lines compared with neighbours to the north and south. Mention however must be made of two spectacular viaducts, one to the east of Accrington and the beautiful 48 arch structure at Whalley between Hellifield and Blackburn.

Happily at the time of writing all survive with the exception of the link between Skipton and Colne and that between Accrington and Bury. None of the routes are intensively used today, indeed the future of the Copy Pit and Hellifield-Blackburn links continues to be the subject of debate. The minimal freight traffic on all of the lines is perhaps a sad commentary on the declining importance of today's railways.

Snow and sunshine combine to make a winter wonderland of the Yorkshire Dales near Bell Busk. Class 47 No. 47533 slips down the 1 in 132 with the four-coach 10.40 Carlisle-Nottingham on 27th December 1984.

Opposite top: A general view of Leeds City station from the west on 18th May 1967 shortly after completion of the modernisation programme. Note the 'Peaks' with small yellow warning panels; the one on the right heading 1M91 the 'up' "Waverley", Edinburgh-St. Pancras.

Opposite, middle and bottom: Two photographs which underline the pace of change on British Rail during the last 20 years. The old order is depicted above, where a 'Peak' is seen approaching Whitehall Junction with the 'up' "Thames-Clyde Express" in July 1965. In the photograph, below, taken 17 years later from almost the same spot, only a few landmarks remain unchanged. Still prominent on the skyline are the two chimneys of Kirkstall Power Station, but even these are likely to be demolished in the near future. Prototype Class 140 4-wheel railcars Nos 140001 and 140002 run into Leeds while undergoing evaluation trials between Ilkley and Leeds on 7th October 1981.

Above: Following the elevation of the route to Anglo-Scottish status with the completion of the S&C, the volume of traffic between Leeds and Shipley justified quadrupling this busy main line, although the work was not completed until 1910. Following a decline in freight traffic and a reduction in the importance of Bradford Forster Square as the city's passenger terminus, rationalisation back to double track status was inevitable. Three months after the two tracks on the left had been abandoned, 'Peak' No. D25 (45021) heads the 'up' "Thames-Clyde Express" through Newlay Cutting on 10th June 1966.

Above: A delightful selection of distant signals adjacent to Shipley Bingley Junction signal box sets the scene for 'Peak' No. D24 (45027) with the 'down' "Waverley" in April 1966. Note the 55A shed code plate in the middle of the small yellow warning panel. The site to the right of the leading coach has since been developed to accommodate a further platform for Shipley station which now has platforms serving each side of the triangle of lines to Leeds, Ilkley, Skipton and Bradford.

Middle: Emerging from Thackley Tunnel on what is now the surviving 'up' line is Class 25 No. D5284 (25134) with a Morecambe-Leeds train on 23rd March 1967. Judging by the ballast, the permanent way on the left, abandoned four days earlier, seems distinctly superior to that retained for further use!

Left: 'A shadow of its former glory' is a well worn cliché but one which is particularly apt when related to Bradford Forster Square station. Once a major rail terminal, today it is host only to local passenger services to Ilkley and Keighley. Even in 1967 atrophy and decay was well advanced but at least parcels and goods traffic were still in evidence. On a very wet 18th March 1967 'Jubilee' 4-6-0 No. 45647 *Sturdee* awaits departure with the 15.20 parcels to Heysham, while 'Britannia' 4-6-2 No. 70025 *Western Star* waits its next turn of duty.

The four-track section of main line between Bingley and Keighley survived until 1966. In this picture, part of the track is still visible alongside the 'up' "Thames-Clyde Express" headed by a Class 25 and a failed 'Peak'. On a site close to the rear of the train a brand new station, Crossflatts, was built on the old trackbed in 1983.

Above: Great Western steam locomotives are rare visitors indeed to the trans-Pennine rail routes. In 1967 'Castle' class No. 7029 *Clun Castle* made a series of excursions to Newcastle and Carlisle. In preparation for these visits No. 7029 is seen here undergoing clearance tests at Keighley on 21st August 1967. No doubt passengers on the passing 'up' express hauled by 'Peak' No. D25 (45021) were more than a little surprised to see a polished copper-capped chimney at Keighley. The line beyond the steam locomotive leads to the Keighley & Worth Valley Railway.

Bingley station has been little modernised over the years and its commodious accommodation is today rather inappropriate for the diesel multiple units which call on their journeys between industrial West Yorkshire, Skipton, Morecambe and Carlisle. Leaving a deserted station on 30th September 1977 is a 2-car Class 105 dmu forming the 09.35 Skipton-Leeds service.

This interesting signal at the east end of Skipton has long since disappeared. 'Peak' No. D34 (45119) at the head of maroon and blue/grey stock is at full power with IM91, the 'up' "Waverley" express on 21st August 1967.

That Skipton was once a rail centre of considerable importance is clearly evident in this busy scene photographed on 23rd March 1967. On the left, 'Jubilee' No. 45593 *Kolhapur* heads the 15.20 Bradford Forster Square-Heysham parcels while on the right, BR Standard Class 4 No. 75058 comes off the Grassington branch with a short freight. Happily, 18 years later the scene has hardly changed – except of course for the motive power!

In this photograph, taken at Skipton on 8th August 1979, Class 31s Nos 31272 and 31409 provide the motive power for a Tilcon company train bound for Hull. In the distance and to the left of the train can be seen the old steam shed, now used as private industrial premises.

Apart from their latter day exploits on the Standedge route hauling York-Liverpool expresses, 'Deltics' have been rare performers on trans-Pennine metals. Most of their appearances were on rail enthusiast excursions. One such being a Peterborough-Leeds-Carlisle tour running over the S&C on 5th December 1981. Looking spick and span in her final month of BR service No. 55015 *Tulyar* heads away from Skipton with the northbound "Hadrian Flyer". The line through to Colne and Blackburn diverged from the main line at this point and part of the trackbed can be seen on the extreme right.

By a strange coincidence the location chosen to photograph the 11.50 Glasgow-Nottingham on 17th April 1981 was also the precise spot where 'Peak' No. 45056 was to fail totally. Stranded passengers had ample time to enjoy the superb spring weather and delightful views of Smardale while assistance was summoned from Carlisle. The rescue locomotive, a Class 47, worked forward wrong line to Kirkby Stephen and reversed to pilot the train forward, some 90 minutes late. Note the open cab doors on the locomotive.

Overleaf top: High above the rooftops of Crosby Garrett, Class 47 No. 47413 disturbs the peace as it speeds through with one of the numerous expresses diverted over the S&C from the West Coast route on 2nd April 1983. A light dusting of snow on the hills would seem to support the local saying "Never cast a clout till May be out".

Overleaf bottom: Helm Tunnel, the first to the south of Appleby, is surprisingly set in undulating rich farming country. Although access by public road or footpath is difficult the views from above the tunnel, both to the north and to the south are quite spectacular. Heading towards the northern portal is Class 40 No. 40013 with the 09.07 Leeds-Carlisle on 7th September 1983.

The English Electric Class 37s have never been regular performers on the S&C, although in recent years they have been used increasingly on the Carlisle-Appleby-Warcop pick-up freight. On 9th August 1984 the then unique 2,000 hp locomotive No. 37292 was employed on this duty and is pictured on the return trip approaching the tunnel at Culgaith.

The depth of the cutting to the north of Newbiggin station dwarfs 'Peak' No. 45072 with a 'down' coal haul on 3rd July 1980. The soft red sandstone, so typical of this locality, can be seen at the bottom left of the picture and its ease of excavation is the probable reason why engineers decided against the construction of yet another tunnel.

143

The photographer's vantage point for the previous picture is quite obvious in this track-level view of Class 40 No. 40094 hard at work with an 'up' freight on 22nd July 1981.

Although Class 27s were synonymous with secondary duties north of the border, they were occasionally to be found at work on the Carlisle-Appleby pick up. On 20th August 1984 No. 27024 was photographed heading south between Langwathby and Culgaith.

Rationalisation is evidently almost complete at Armathwaite. It is however easy to appreciate the once generous accommodation provided to deal with local freight traffic. The only modern building in sight is the extension to the station building which is used by the local branch of the British Legion. Note the soot deposits on the goods warehouse, a permanent reminder of the line's steam operated past. Class 40 No. 40193 passes by with the Appleby-Carlisle freight on 9th September 1983.

Chapter 9

The Stainmore Line

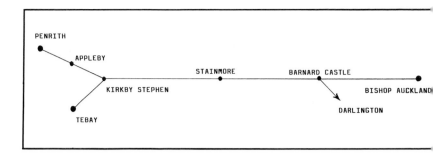

The two northernmost trans-Pennine lines were adopted by the North Eastern Railway and both are quite distinctive in character, not least because the Newcastle-Carlisle and the Stainmore route were constructed without recourse to major tunnel works. A fact all the more surprising when it is noted that the Stainmore route, at 1,378 feet above sea level, was the highest of all the trans-Pennine lines; the virtual absence of tunnels though was more than compensated by several magnificent viaducts, those at Deepdale and Belah being particularly worthy of note.

The Stainmore line traversed bleak high moorland country serving in its entirety scant rural communities. Clearly local traffic was not the raison d'etre of the railway; the line's fortunes were closely allied to the lucrative coal and coke traffic from the coalfields of the North East to the iron and steel industries around Barrow and Millom. In the west the line bifurcated to the west of Kirkby Stephen; the southern route connected with the LNWR at Tebay and eventually took its separate way again to the Cumbrian coast at Hincaster Junction. The rural northern cross country route terminated at Penrith. In the East, Barnard Castle was the focal point of lines from Bishop Auckland and Darlington, along with a branch from Middleton-in-Teesdale.

The railway was never a prime passenger carrier, indeed in this context in later years its infrequent moments of glory were on a few summer Saturdays when it carried holiday traffic to and from the Lancashire coastal resorts.

Along with the Cromford and High Peak, way to the south, motive power on the Stainmore line never fully benefited from the post Beeching modernisation programme. Multiple units were drafted in to operate the sparse passenger traffic in the final years but there are few recorded occasions (and even fewer photographs) of diesel locomotives working trains over the line. Sadly this superb railway closed as a through route on 22nd January 1962.

Below: A Class 101 dmu rolls into Barnard Castle forming the 16.34 Darlington-Penrith service on 14th October 1961. Visible in the distance is the signal box and level crossing at the east end of the station. At one time a turntable and a small two-road locomotive shed were sited to the north of the line just beyond the crossing.

(Hugh Ballantyne)

Bottom: The North Eastern Railway's trans Pennine railway over Stainmore Summit was never a major rail artery, although it carried vast quantities of freight traffic at the turn of the century. Passenger trains continued to operate over part of the line until the mid 1960s when the service from Darlington was finally withdrawn on 28th November 1964. Barnard Castle station is depicted in 1966, by which time all track and fittings had been removed. Note the diminutive train shed, a feature of so many North Eastern stations.

The RCTS commemorative rail tour "The Stainmore Limited" is pictured traversing the West Auckland–Barnard Castle section of the line near Cockfield, westbound for Tebay on 20th January 1962. Providing the motive power are nicely groomed BR Standard 2-6-0s Nos 77003 and 76049.

(R.H. Leslie)

At 1,370ft above sea level Stainmore Summit was the highest point reached by a trans-Pennine railway; over 200ft higher than the celebrated summit of the Midland at Ais Gill. Inevitably the gradients of the line and the extremes of winter weather were the railwaymen's principal adversaries; indeed in the great freeze of 1947 the line was totally blocked by snow for no less than eight weeks. Here the summit is bathed in summer sunshine as BR Standard Class 2 2-6-0s Nos 78017 and 78013 pass Stainmore signal box with a string of 14 mineral wagons and a brake van, bound for Bishop Auckland on 16th August 1961.

(Gavin Morrison)

Surprisingly few photographs have come to light of the short reign of diesel multiple units on passenger services over the line. When this picture was taken on 14th October 1961 through services were to last just another ten weeks. A 3-car Class 101 Metro-Cammell set, looking very smart with its 'whisker' decorative panel at the front, waits in vain for passengers at the weed-covered platforms of Barras, forming the 10.52 Darlington-Penrith service.

(Hugh Ballantyne)

The most impressive engineering structure on the line was Belah Viaduct just one mile to the west of Barras station. Ivatt Class 4 2-6-0 No. 43015 pounds up the 1 in 60 over the steel structure with the 11.05 Summer SO Blackpool-South Shields on 18th July 1959. At its highest point the track was 196ft above the river below. The viaduct was demolished in 1963, although the shell of the signal box seen at the extreme left of the picture was still standing in the Summer of 1986.

(R.H. Leslie)

To the railway enthusiast the North Eastern scene at Kirkby Stephen was much more interesting than the bleak aspect offered by the Midland at their West station. In addition to the well appointed station, which even boasted an electrically operated lift, using electricity generated from a nearby mini hydro-electric plant, there was a delightful four-road locomotive shed and a small, but quite busy, goods yard.

Top: Kirkby Stephen East station as seen from the west on 23rd August 1953.

(Ken Plant)

Right: Residents of Kirkby Stephen shed photographed on the same date included Ivatt Class 2 2-6-0s Nos 46476/7/8/80/1 along with vintage Class J25 0-6-0s Nos 65655/73/95 and Class J21 0-6-0 No. 65100.

(Ken Plant)

Below: Except for a brief spell in 1955, when a pair of Class Q6 0-8-0s were shedded here, small six coupled engines were the mainstay of the line's motive power. Towards the end the older NER 0-6-0s were displaced by BR Standard 2-6-0 types augmented by Ivatt Class 4MT Moguls. Standard 2-6-0s Nos 77003 and 76049 provided the motive power for the very last passenger train to traverse the line on 20th January 1962. In this splendid study the pair are pictured leaving Kirkby Stephen for Tebay.

(Gavin Morrison)

At the time of writing the Appleby East-Warcop branch is the only surviving section of the line – courtesy of the Ministry of Defence. Freight trains run on an as-required basis; normally at least one train being required each week. At infrequent intervals, and often in the early hours of the morning, troop specials add a little extra interest as in this scene to the east of Appleby. Class 40 No. 40099 cautiously eases a nine-coach Stranraer-Warcop army special down the branch on 2nd June 1984.

(Gavin Morrison)

The North Eastern joined the London & North Western main line at Eden Vale Junction to the south of Penrith. Class 3MT 2-6-2T No. 82027 swings away from the West Coast route with the 14.57 Penrith-Darlington on 6th August 1956. Today the scene has changed totally with the advent of 25kV electrification and the complete obliteration of the junction.

(R.H. Leslie)

Slotting in between exotic locomotives, such as 'Duchesses' and 'Royal Scots' at the head of WCML expresses, a 5-car Class 101 Metro-Cammell unit ambles south from Penrith towards Eden Vale Junction, with the 15.05 service to Darlington on 15th August 1959.

(R.H. Leslie)

Chapter 10

The Newcastle & Carlisle Route

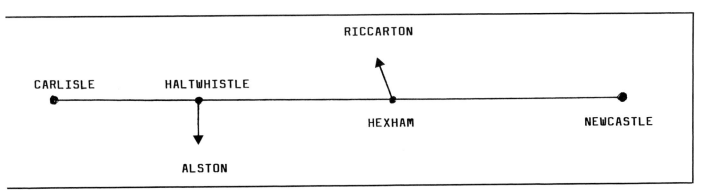

The Newcastle & Carlisle Railway, later passing into North Eastern Railway ownership, crosses England's narrowest neck and, discounting the Cromford and High Peak with its rope-worked inclines, was the first trans-Pennine railway. In a way its inclusion here as a trans-Pennine link is something of a misnomer since the line follows a relatively natural break along the South Tyne, Irthing and Eden Valleys with the Southern Uplands of Scotland to the north and the Pennines to the south.

The first section of the N&C, between Newcastle and Blaydon, was opened to passenger traffic on 9th March 1835 and as a through route to Carlisle on 18th June 1838. In its heyday the line boasted a dual exit from Newcastle, on the north and south banks of the Tyne to Wylam, several branches and, at Hexham, a link with the Border Counties Railway. All are now closed and lifted, the final casualty being the Alston branch in April 1976.

Contrast in heights of semaphore signals at the east end of Hexham station. On a delightful autumn afternoon a 2-car Class 101 dmu is pictured forming a local service to Newcastle on 5th December 1983.

Scenically the line is pleasant rather than spectacular while connoisseurs of rail travel will find little to raise the pulse rate; the summit is more accurately defined as a six mile plateau, the gradients (with exception of one stretch near How Mill) modest in the extreme and there are few engineering features of note.

Apart from the industrial section between Newcastle and Blaydon, the line serves the sparsely populated hinterland of the Northern Fells. More significantly it is a direct and very convenient link between the two major north-south rail arteries, the East Coast and West Coast routes. As recently as 1979 its value as a diversionary route was fully appreciated with the ECML north of Newcastle was closed because of the Penmanshiel Tunnel disaster. As long as there is a reasonably comprehensive BR network, by reasons of geography one cannot envisage a rail-less gap between Newcastle and Carlisle.

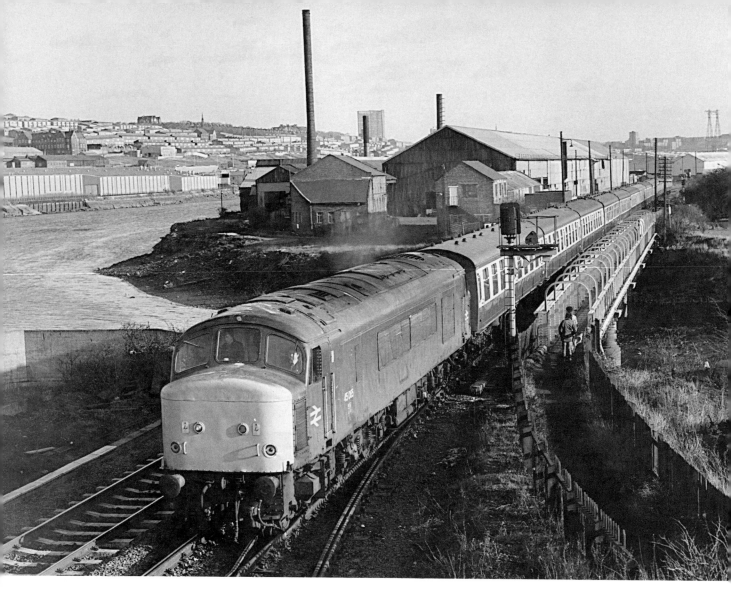

'Peak' No. 45065 hugs the south bank of the Tyne at Derwenthaugh, once a location of intense industrial activity, with the 12.35 Newcastle to Carlisle football excursion on 20th November 1982.

(Peter J. Robinson)

The Newcastle-Carlisle line was the first of the trans-Pennine lines to be approved for the operation of steam-hauled railtours following the lifting of the ban in October 1971. In the event, the route has not proved to be particularly popular although a notable visitor on 16th March 1985 was former LMS Pacific No. 46229 *Duchess of Hamilton*, seen here westbound at Blaydon making for more familiar territory at Carlisle.

A Metro-Cammell Class 101 dmu forming a Hexham-Newcastle service passes Stella South Power Station near Blaydon on 10th June 1976.

(Peter J. Robinson)

Passing the site of the junction at West Wylam for the Wylam loop, which until 1968 took the north bank of the Tyne through Newburn and Scotswood to Newcastle Central, is 'Deltic' No. 55008 *The Green Howards* with the diverted 05.50 King's Cross-Aberdeen on 7th July 1979. It is pleasing to note that the splendid bridge over the River Tyne still finds a use in 1986, even if only for pedestrians.

(Peter J. Robinson)

Class 31 No. 31319 and Class 37 No. 37001 make an unusual pairing as they head east through Prudhoe with the Dalston-Teesport empty tanks on 7th July 1979.

(*Peter J. Robinson*)

Below: The North Eastern Railway was a prime mover of coal and coal drops were extensively used for distribution from railhead to domestic and industrial consumers. Surprisingly those at Hexham survive intact and are a pleasant reminder of a bygone era. Photographed on 5th September 1983.

Opposite top: One of the more interesting features of the Newcastle-Carlisle line is, in the 1980s, the number of surviving relics from North Eastern Railway days. Few travellers on the line can fail to notice the signal boxes at Wylam and Hexham. Both are fine structures built upon brick piers and a steel superstructure which spans the running lines, but of the two perhaps Hexham is the more impressive. Seen through the supporting ironmongery is Class 47 No. 47051 with the 15.38 Carlisle-Edinburgh on 5th September 1983. Hexham station can just be discerned in the middle distance.

Opposite bottom: Wylam signal box enjoys an elevated position to the west of the level crossing adjacent to the station. The signalman enjoys superb views of both road and railway. The usual level crossing gates have been replaced by lifting barriers and the long term future of the box itself is far from assured. A Cravens Class 105 2-car unit forming a Hexham-Newcastle service slows for the station on 5th September 1983.